Crafts to Make in the Winter

CRAFTS FOR ALL SEASONS

Crafts
to make
in the
Winter

KATHY ROSS

illustrated by Vicky Enright

The Millbrook Press   Brookfield, Connecticut

To Shawn, who enjoys all the seasons! —K.R.

For my sister, Andy, who's always there for me with a big heart.—V.E.

Library of Congress Cataloging-in-Publication Data
Ross, Kathy (Katharine Reynolds), 1948–
Crafts to make in the winter / Kathy Ross; illustrated by Vicky Enright.
p.   cm. —(Crafts for all seasons)
Summary: Presents instructions for creating twenty-nine craft projects with a winter or holiday theme,
including a confetti noise maker, Christmas candy ornament, baggy snowman, lace snowflake, bird
valentine, and more.
ISBN 0-7613-0319-7 (lib. bdg.). — ISBN 0-7613-0336-7 (pbk.)
1. Handicraft—Juvenile literature. 2. Winter—Juvenile literature. [1. Handicraft.] I. Enright, Vicky, ill.
II. Title. III. Series: Ross, Kathy (Katharine Reynolds). 1948– Crafts for all seasons.
TT160.R7142293   1999
745.5—dc21   98-43573   CIP   AC

Published by The Millbrook Press, Inc.
2 Old New Milford Road
Brookfield, Connecticut 06804
Visit us at our Web site: http://www.millbrookpress.com

Contents

For many people the coming of winter means lots of snow.

Snowman Pin

Here is what you need:

 margarine tub for mixing

 white glue

 white poster paint and a paintbrush

 peanut

Styrofoam tray for drying

scissors

tablespoon

salt

black and orange construction paper scraps

ruler

red yarn

safety pin

Here is what you do:

1 In the margarine tub, mix a few drops of glue into a tablespoon of white paint. Paint the peanut white for the body of the snowman. Sprinkle the wet paint with salt and lean the peanut against the edge of the Styrofoam tray to dry.

2 Cut a hat, eyes, and buttons for the snowman from the black paper. Cut a carrot nose from the orange paper. Glue the pieces onto the peanut snowman.

3 Cut a 5-inch (13-cm) piece of red yarn. Tie the yarn around the peanut snowman to make a scarf. Secure the scarf with glue. Trim the ends to a length that looks right for your snowman.

4 Slip the back of a safety pin through the yarn scarf at the back of the snowman.

Wear this little snowman on your coat or shirt. This snowman is happy indoors or out.

7)

Even if it doesn't snow where you live, you can make a snowman.

Jar Snowman

Here is what you need:

 large plastic jar with lid

 fiberfill

four buttons

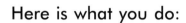 two twigs

 scissors

orange felt scrap

large red pom-pom

 white glue

 masking tape

Here is what you do:

1 Soak the jar in warm water to remove the label and any excess glue.

2 Stuff the jar with fiberfill to make the body of the snowman.

3 Slip two buttons between the side of the jar and the fiberfill for the snowman's buttons. Cut a nose from the orange felt and slip it in the jar above the buttons. Put two more buttons above the nose for the eyes. Slip a twig into each side of the jar for the arms of the snowman.

4 Put the lid on the jar. Put a small piece of masking tape on the top center of the lid to create a better gluing surface. Glue the pom-pom in the center of the lid to make it look like a winter hat.

You might want to use cut paper or small stones for your snowman's eyes and buttons.

9)

Decorated Holiday Plates

Here is what you need:

 colorful holiday plates for your favorite holiday

 ruler

   sequins, trims, glitter, cotton balls, and other collage materials

 hole punch

scissors

 thin ribbon in a color that looks nice with the plate picture

white glue

Here is what you do:

1 Choose decorations to trim the picture on your holiday plate. Use decorations that will highlight the picture printed on the plate. If you have a Santa picture, you could cover the beard with cotton. If you have a dreidel picture, you might want to decorate the design with silver and blue glitter and trims. If you are decorating a Kwanzaa plate, you can bring out the picture with a selection of materials in red, green, and black, the colors of Kwanzaa.

10)

2 Punch a hole in the top of the plate. Cut a 5-inch (13-cm) length of ribbon. String the ribbon through the hole and tie the two ends together to make a hanger.

Each plate picture will be a unique creation.

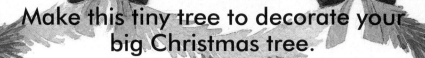

Make this tiny tree to decorate your big Christmas tree.

Tiny Tree Ornament

Here is what you need:

 green yarn

scissors

ruler

craft stick

white glue

Styrofoam tray for drying

red felt scrap

colorful round- and star-shaped sequins

green rickrack

Here is what you do:

1 Wrap green yarn around your hand about thirty times. Slide the yarn off your hand and cut the end off from the main ball of yarn. Cut through the yarn loops twice so that you have two equal bunches of yarn.

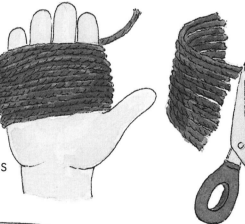

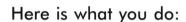

2 Cut a 6-inch (15-cm)-long piece of yarn. Glue the two ends of the yarn about half way down one side of the craft stick so that a loop forms a hanger at one end of the stick.

Christmas Ornaments

3 Rub glue all over one side of the craft stick. Lay the stick down on the tray and glue one of the piles of yarn strands across all of the stick except for one inch at the bottom. Turn the stick over and cover the other side in the same way, using the second pile of yarn. Let the glue dry.

4 Trim the yarn on each side to form a triangle-shaped tree. Rub glue over both sides of the tree and glue the trimmed-off bits of yarn back onto the tree to make it look shaggy.

5 Cut a base for each side of the tree from the red felt. Glue the two felt pieces together with the stick in the middle.

6 Choose one side of the tree to be the front of the ornament. Decorate the tree with the round- and star- shaped sequins. Decorate the red felt base with rickrack.

You might have some other ideas for how you want to trim your tree ornament.

13)

Make this Christmas tree with personality to sit on your shelf this holiday season.

Box Corner Christmas Tree

Here is what you need:

 large-size cereal box

 scissors

 pencil

large red pom-pom

 green, white, and black construction paper

sequins

white glue

cellophane tape

red marker

old Christmas card with a written greeting inside

 four 12-inch (30-cm) green glitter stems

Here is what you do:

1 Cut the corner from the bottom of the box so that the side of the box is the same length as the bottom of the box. The open side of the triangle will be the bottom of the tree.

2 Use the pencil to trace around one side of the tree on the green paper. Cut around the tracing, leaving an extra inch of paper on each long side. Cut a second piece of paper of the same size to cover the other side of the triangle tree.

14)

3 Cover the entire outside edge of the triangle tree with glue. Glue green paper over each side, folding the extra paper down over the sides of the box. Trim off any extra paper.

4 Glue a triangle of green paper to the front and back of the tree.

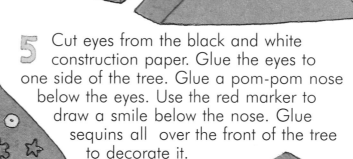

5 Cut eyes from the black and white construction paper. Glue the eyes to one side of the tree. Glue a pom-pom nose below the eyes. Use the red marker to draw a smile below the nose. Glue sequins all over the front of the tree to decorate it.

6 Poke a hole in each side of the tree. Put an end of a sparkle stem through each hole to make arms for the tree. Secure the ends of the sparkle stems inside the box with cellophane tape. Cut a greeting from the inside of an old Christmas card. Tape the ends of the two arms together behind the greeting to look like the tree is holding the greeting.

7 Tape the ends of two sparkle stems inside the bottom of the triangle tree. Bend the two stems out to form legs. Bend the stems in the middle to form knees, then forward at the ends to shape feet.

I bet this happy little tree will put everyone who sees it in the Christmas spirit.

15)

Turn old lipstick tops into charming little trims for the Christmas tree.

Christmas Candy Ornament

Here is what you need:

gold lipstick top

green yarn or thin ribbon

scissors

clear plastic wrap

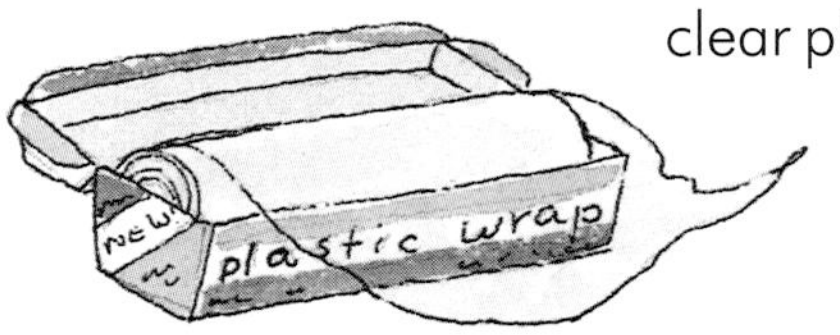

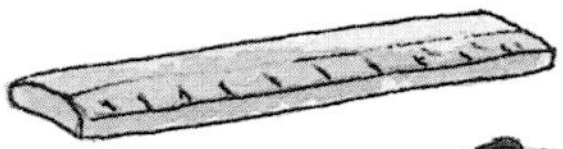

ruler

red or gold string or embroidery floss

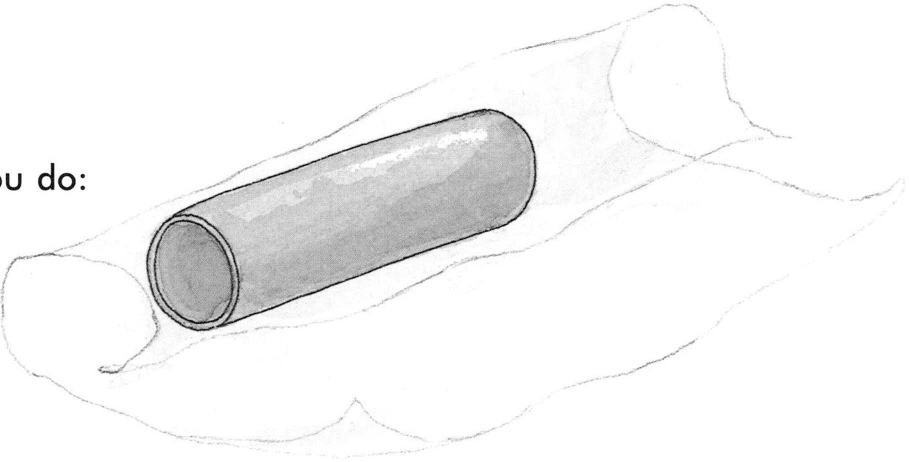

Here is what you do:

1 Wrap the gold lipstick top in a piece of clear plastic wrap.

2 Tie each open end of the wrap closed with a piece of pretty ribbon or yarn tied in a bow.

3 Trim the ends of the plastic wrap so that they are even.

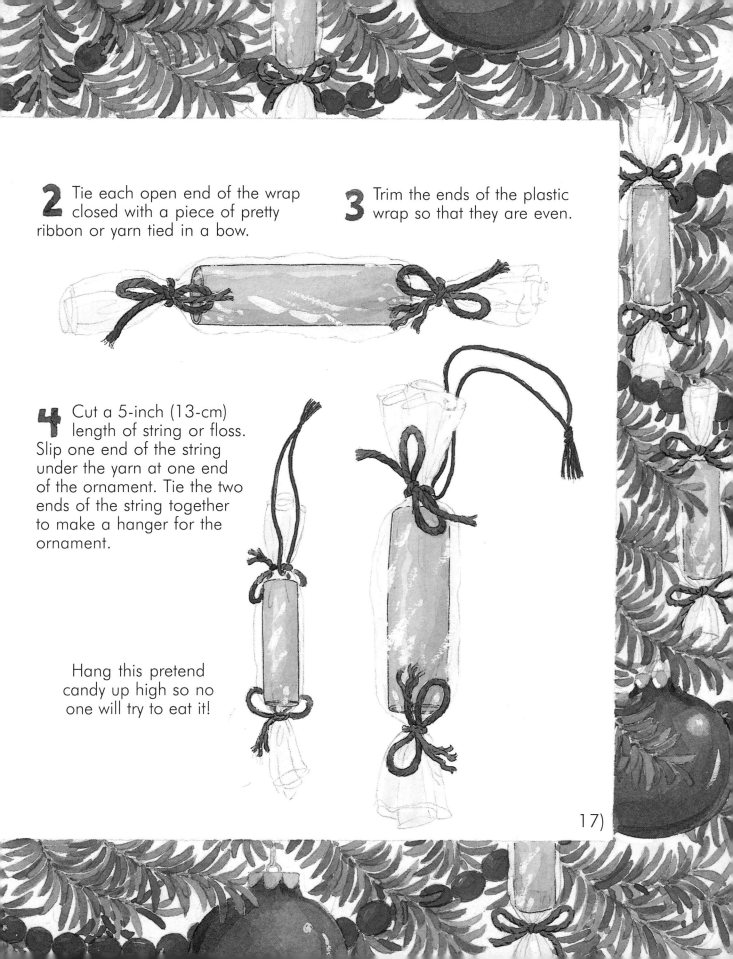

4 Cut a 5-inch (13-cm) length of string or floss. Slip one end of the string under the yarn at one end of the ornament. Tie the two ends of the string together to make a hanger for the ornament.

Hang this pretend candy up high so no one will try to eat it!

Reindeer Puppet

Here is what you need:

ruler

scissors

old necktie

gold sparkle stem

white glue

white and black construction paper scraps

large red pom-pom

Here is what you do:

1 Measuring from the point of the wide end of the tie, cut a 10-inch (25-cm)-long piece from the end of the tie. Make sure you can slip your hand into the tie between the front of the tie and the liner, so that you can work the puppet. If the liner is sewn to the tie in such a way that you cannot get your hand all the way through, just snip the threads that are blocking the way.

2 Measuring from the point, cut a 6-inch (15-cm)-long piece from the narrow end of the same tie. Trim the cut end of the piece into a point to match the point on the other end.

3 Cut two 1-inch (2.5-cm) slits in the front of the tie about 5 inches (13 cm) up from the point and 2 inches (5 cm) apart. Slip the narrow cut end of the tie through the slits so that the ends form two ears.

4 Cut an 8-inch (20-cm)-long piece from the sparkle stem. Slip one end of the stem through the two slits behind the ear piece, then bend the two ends of the sparkle stem up to form antlers. Cut the remaining piece of sparkle stem in half. Wrap a piece around the top part of each antler to form the points of the antler.

5 Cut eyes from the black and white paper scraps. Glue the eyes in place below the ears.

6 Glue the red pom-pom on the point of the tie for the nose.

Does that red nose make you think of a very special reindeer?

19)

Make this banner to decorate your house for the Hanukkah season.

Dreidel Banner

Here is what you need:

scissors

ruler

blue and silver trims

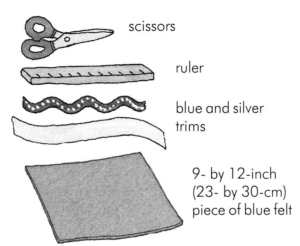

9- by 12-inch (23- by 30-cm) piece of blue felt

cereal box cardboard

two silver sparkle stems

white glue

two old neckties

large gold or silver sequins

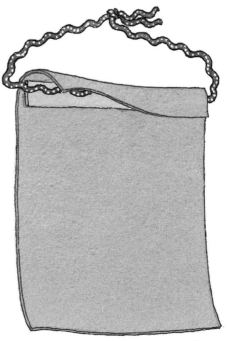

Here is what you do:

1 Cut a 1½-inch (3-cm)-wide strip of cardboard 9 inches (23 cm) long to form a support for the top of the banner. Cut a piece of trim about 2 feet (60 cm) long and tie the ends together to form a hanger for the banner. Fold one 9-inch side of the felt over the hanger and the cardboard support and glue them in place.

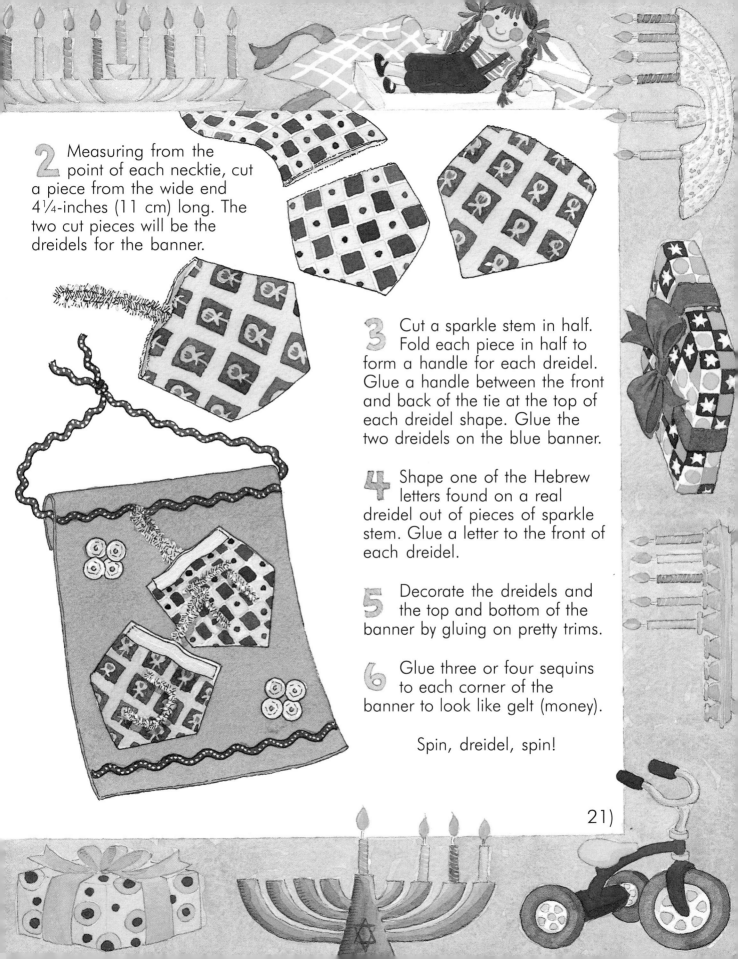

2 Measuring from the point of each necktie, cut a piece from the wide end 4¼-inches (11 cm) long. The two cut pieces will be the dreidels for the banner.

3 Cut a sparkle stem in half. Fold each piece in half to form a handle for each dreidel. Glue a handle between the front and back of the tie at the top of each dreidel shape. Glue the two dreidels on the blue banner.

4 Shape one of the Hebrew letters found on a real dreidel out of pieces of sparkle stem. Glue a letter to the front of each dreidel.

5 Decorate the dreidels and the top and bottom of the banner by gluing on pretty trims.

6 Glue three or four sequins to each corner of the banner to look like gelt (money).

Spin, dreidel, spin!

Make a corn magnet for Kwanzaa.

Ear of Corn Magnet

Here is what you need:

- scissors
- ruler
- small-size bubble wrap
- margarine tub and craft stick for mixing
- sticky-back magnet
- water
- cereal box cardboard
- yellow and brown tissue paper
- white glue
- Styrofoam tray for drying

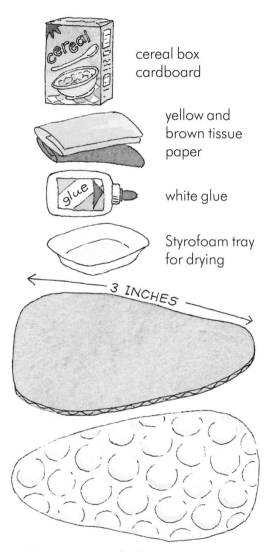

3 INCHES

Here is what you do:

1 Cut a 3-inch (8-cm) -tall corn shape from the cardboard.

2 Cut a piece of bubble wrap to fit over one side of the corn shape to make the corn kernels.

3 Mix three parts of glue to one part of water in the margarine tub and mix with the craft stick.

22)

4 Cut some strips of brown tissue paper about 2½ inches (6 cm) long and about 1 inch (2½ cm) wide. Glue the strips sticking out from the top of the corn to form the husks.

5 Cover the front of the corn with glue and glue the bubble wrap to the corn shape, covering the bottom edges of the brown husks.

6 Cut a piece of yellow tissue paper large enough to wrap around the corn shape to cover the front and the back of the corn. Dip the yellow tissue paper in the watery glue, then wrap it around the corn to cover it.
Let the project dry completely on the Styrofoam tray.

7 Put a piece of sticky-back magnet on the back of the corn.

You might want to make your mom an ear of corn magnet for each child in your family.

23)

Confetti Noise Maker

Here is what you need:

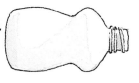
small plastic detergent bottle

scissors

thin ribbon

confetti

three or more jingle bells

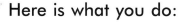
ruler

Here is what you do:

1 Cut an 18-inch (46-cm) piece of ribbon. String three or more jingle bells onto the ribbon. Tie the ribbon and bells around the bottle. Tie the two ends of the ribbon together to make a wrist hanger for the bottle.

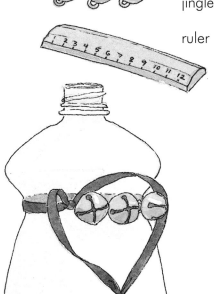

24

2 Fill the bottle with confetti.

Bring in the new year by shaking your bottle to ring the bells and toss the confetti.

Cold winter weather means ice skating.

Ice Skater

Here is what you need:

markers

scissors

tongue depressor

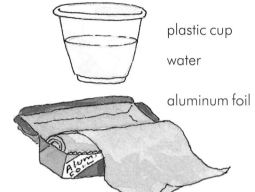

plastic cup

water

aluminum foil

Here is what you do:

1 Use the markers to turn the tongue depressor into the figure of an ice skater.

2 Fill the plastic cup half full of water.

3 Cover the open top of the cup with a piece of aluminum foil.

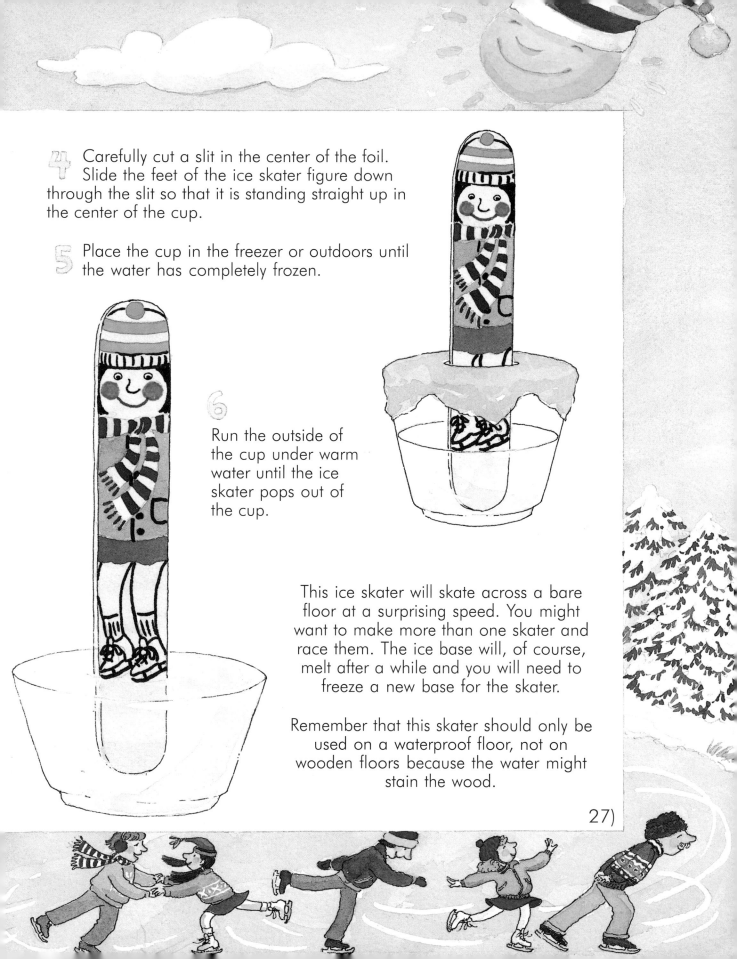

4. Carefully cut a slit in the center of the foil. Slide the feet of the ice skater figure down through the slit so that it is standing straight up in the center of the cup.

5. Place the cup in the freezer or outdoors until the water has completely frozen.

6. Run the outside of the cup under warm water until the ice skater pops out of the cup.

This ice skater will skate across a bare floor at a surprising speed. You might want to make more than one skater and race them. The ice base will, of course, melt after a while and you will need to freeze a new base for the skater.

Remember that this skater should only be used on a waterproof floor, not on wooden floors because the water might stain the wood.

27)

This little snowman belongs indoors, not outdoors.

Baggy Snowman

Here is what you need:

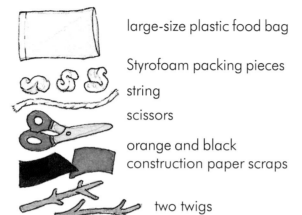

large-size plastic food bag

Styrofoam packing pieces

string

scissors

orange and black construction paper scraps

two twigs

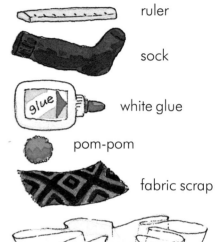

ruler

sock

white glue

pom-pom

fabric scrap

Here is what you do:

1. Fill the bottom half of the bag with Styrofoam pieces. Tie the bag closed with string to form the base of the snowman.

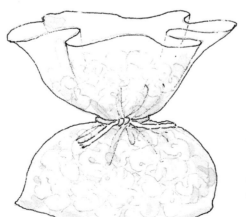

2. Fill the upper part of the bag with enough Styrofoam pieces to make a head for the snowman that is smaller than the body.

3 Cut two eyes for the snowman from black paper. Cut a carrot nose from the orange paper. Arrange the face pieces inside the bag on one side to form a face for the snowman. Tie the top of the bag shut.

4 Poke a twig into each side of the snowman's body to make arms.

5 Cut a 3-inch (8-cm) piece from the toe of the sock to make a hat for the snowman. Put the hat over the top of the snowman's head. Glue the pom-pom to the top of the hat.

6 Cut a scarf for the snowman from the fabric scrap. Tie the scarf around the snowman's neck.

This snowman may be so light that it will tumble away at the slightest breeze, but at least it will never melt!

29)

By January it is hard for the winter birds to find food on their own.

Bird in the Snow Table Decoration

Here is what you need:

clear plastic cup

forked twig small enough to fit inside the cup

 Styrofoam packing worm

two tiny wiggle eyes

cereal box cardboard

white glue

scissors

blue poster paint and a paintbrush

birdseed

blue and yellow construction paper scraps

fiberfill

Styrofoam tray for drying

masking tape

blue trim

pencil

Here is what you do:

1 Carefully slide one branch of the twig through one end of the Styrofoam piece. Tip the piece up to look like a bird perched on a branch. Do this before you paint the bird because you might split the Styrofoam and need to use another one. Secure the perched bird with glue.

2 Paint the bird blue. Let the project dry on the Styrofoam tray.

30)

RECYCLING
Town of Arde

3 Cut wings for the bird from the blue paper and a beak from the yellow paper. Glue the wings to the back of the bird. Glue the beak on the head of the bird. Glue two wiggle eyes above the beak.

4 Trace around the open end of the cup on the cardboard. Cut out the traced circle.

5 Glue the fiberfill to the circle for snow. Glue the branch with the bird on top of the snow. Glue some birdseed in the snow.

6 Cover the rim of the cup with masking tape to create a better gluing surface. Put glue around the opening of the cup and glue it over the bird in the snow.

7 Cover the masking tape around the bottom of the cup with glue, then decorate it with trim.

What a pretty reminder to feed the birds!

31)

The birthday of Martin Luther King Jr. is in January.

Martin Luther King Day Banner

Here is what you need:

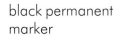 ruler

scissors

 9- by 12-inch
(23- by 30-cm)
piece of white felt

yarn

 black permanent
marker

 cereal box cardboard

 white glue

 poster paint in two
different skin shades
and a paintbrush

newspaper to work on

Here is what you do:

1 Cut a 1½-inch (3¾-cm)-wide strip of cardboard 9 inches (23 cm) long to form a support for the top of the banner. Cut a 2-foot (60-cm) length of yarn and tie the ends together to make a hanger for the banner. Fold one of the 9-inch sides of the felt over the yarn hanger and the cardboard support and glue them in place.

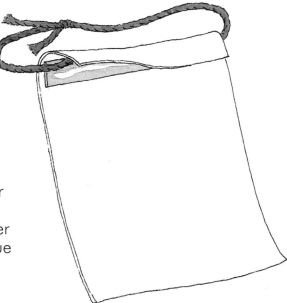

2 Paint your palm one of the skin colors. Carefully make a handprint going up from the bottom of the banner.

3 Paint the other palm a different skin color. Carefully make a second handprint coming down from the top of the banner and just touching the other handprint. Let the paint dry.

4 Use the marker to write the words on your banner that Martin Luther King said: "I have a dream."

Do you know what Martin Luther King's dream was?

"I have a dream"

JOBS FOR ALL

FULL Employment NOW

END RACISM NOW

JOBS FOR ALL

END SEGREGATION NOW

EQUAL RIGHTS NOW

33)

Martin Luther King Jr. wanted people of all races to get along together.

Friends Pin

Here is what you need:

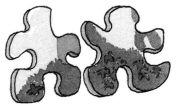 old puzzle pieces

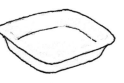 Styrofoam tray for drying

 brown and pink poster paint (or two different colors for skin tones) and a paintbrush

 masking tape

 white glue

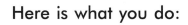 pin backing

Here is what you do:

1 Find two puzzle pieces that look like little people with a round head on top, arms on each side, and legs at the bottom.

2 Paint each piece a different skin color. Let the pieces dry on the Styrofoam tray.

34)

3 Glue the two pieces together to look like they are holding hands.

4 Wrap some masking tape around the back of the pin backing to make a better gluing surface. Glue the pin backing to the back of the joined puzzle pieces.

Wear your friends pin for Martin Luther King Day.

Bring Big Foot to your neighborhood this winter.

Large Tracks

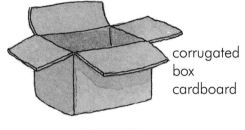

Here is what you need:

 pencil

scissors

 clear packing tape

corrugated box cardboard

 ruler

twine

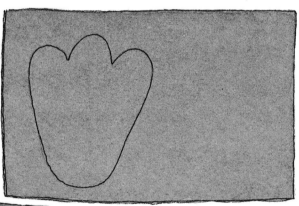

Here is what you do:

1 Draw a large foot shape on the cardboard. Don't make it too huge or it may bend in the snow and not leave a good print. Cut the shape out.

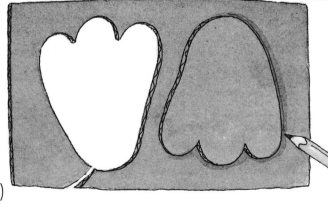

2 Trace around the first foot shape on the cardboard to make a second one. Cut the second one out.

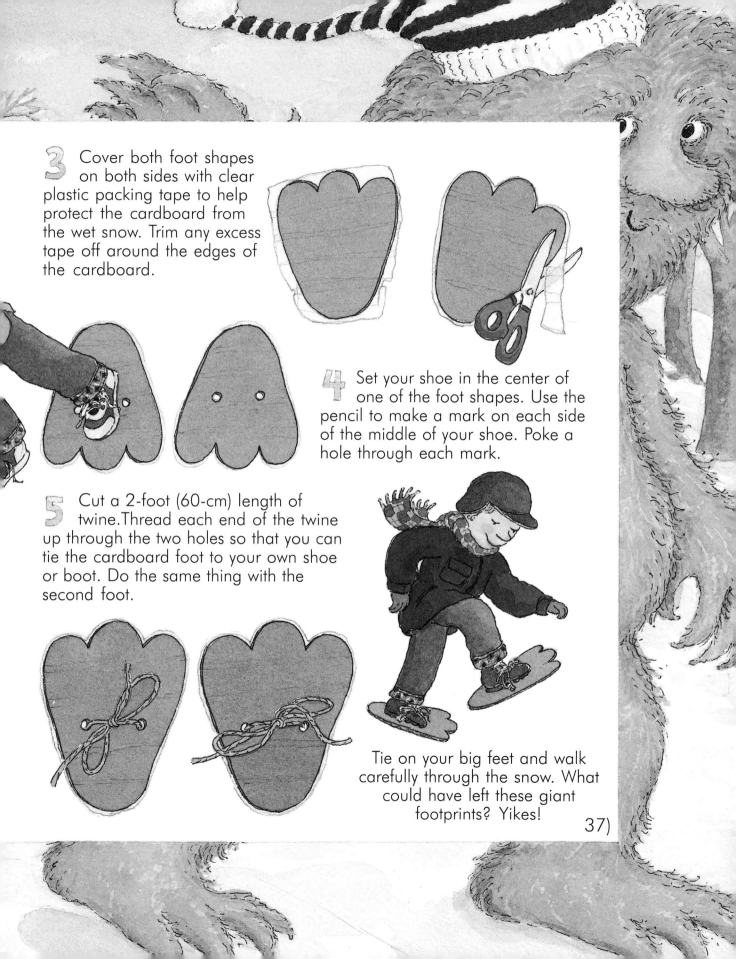

3 Cover both foot shapes on both sides with clear plastic packing tape to help protect the cardboard from the wet snow. Trim any excess tape off around the edges of the cardboard.

4 Set your shoe in the center of one of the foot shapes. Use the pencil to make a mark on each side of the middle of your shoe. Poke a hole through each mark.

5 Cut a 2-foot (60-cm) length of twine. Thread each end of the twine up through the two holes so that you can tie the cardboard foot to your own shoe or boot. Do the same thing with the second foot.

Tie on your big feet and walk carefully through the snow. What could have left these giant footprints? Yikes!

37)

Lace Snowflake

Here is what you need:

ruler

white lace

scissors

white yarn or string

thin white lace
ribbon

white glue

water

margarine tub and
craft stick for mixing

Styrofoam tray

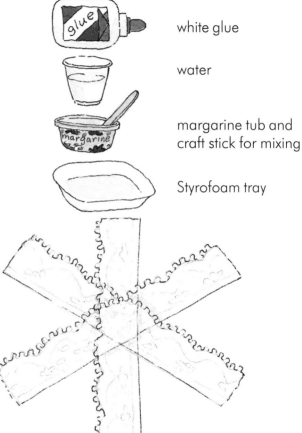

Here is what you do:

1 Cut three 6-inch (15-cm)-long
pieces of lace. Arrange the lace
in a crisscross pattern like a wheel
to make the six points of the
snowflake.

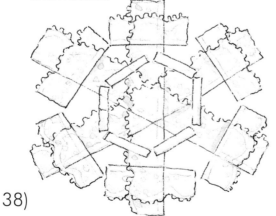

2 Cut smaller pieces of lace
ribbon and yarn to put across the
points of the snowflake. (Remember,
each snowflake is different, and there
are many possibilities. You will want to
experiment with your own design.)

38)

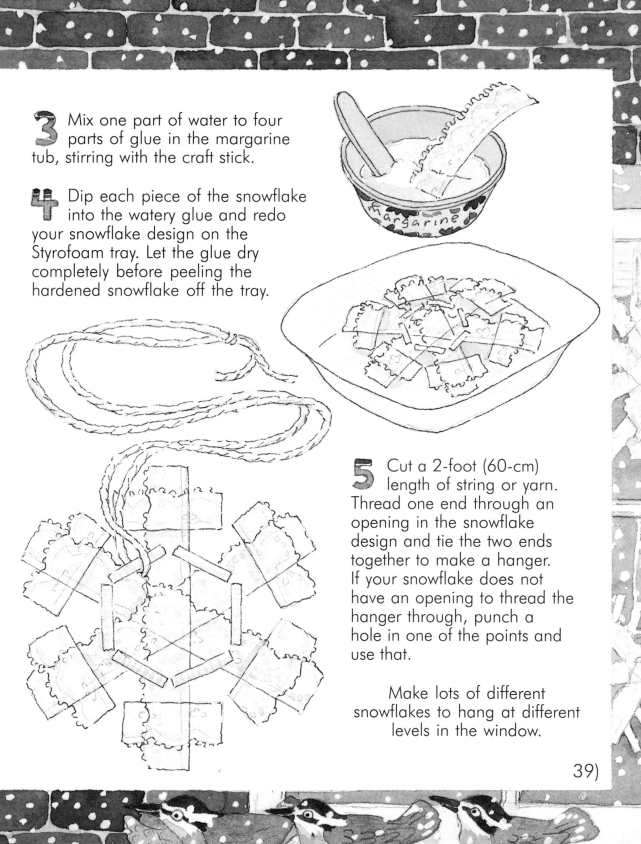

3 Mix one part of water to four parts of glue in the margarine tub, stirring with the craft stick.

4 Dip each piece of the snowflake into the watery glue and redo your snowflake design on the Styrofoam tray. Let the glue dry completely before peeling the hardened snowflake off the tray.

5 Cut a 2-foot (60-cm) length of string or yarn. Thread one end through an opening in the snowflake design and tie the two ends together to make a hanger. If your snowflake does not have an opening to thread the hanger through, punch a hole in one of the points and use that.

Make lots of different snowflakes to hang at different levels in the window.

39)

These lucky birds have their very own feeder.

Hungry Birds Puppet

Here is what you need:

 newspaper to work on

scissors

 two blue feather fluffs

 6-inch (15-cm) paper plate

 old knit glove

cardboard toilet tissue tube

 blue poster paint and a paintbrush

 white glue

birdseed

6-inch (15-cm) paper bowl

blue and orange felt scraps

Here is what you do:

1 Paint the top (eating side) of the paper plate blue. Paint the outside of the cardboard tube blue. Let the paint dry.

2 Glue the tube upright in the center of the plate. Glue the bottom of the bowl to the top of the tube to form a bowl for the bird feeder.

40)

3 Cut the two fingers next to the thumb out of the glove, leaving them attached at the base of each finger.

4 Cut two finger-size holes in the side of the bowl of the feeder. Put the glove fingers on your fingers and push them through each hole. Each finger will be a bird.

5 Cut a beak for each bird from the orange felt. Glue a beak on each bird on the side of the glove finger facing down into the feeder.

6 Cut eyes and wings for each bird from the blue felt and glue them in place.

7 Glue a fluff on the back of each bird for a tail.

8 Rub the bottom of the bowl of the feeder with glue, then sprinkle it with birdseed.

To use the bird feeder puppet, just slip a finger into each little bird and help them peck at the seeds in the bottom of the feeder.

41)

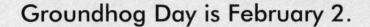

Pop-up Groundhog Puppet

Here is what you need:

scissors

adult-size brown sock

1-foot (30-cm) stick or dowel

white glue

2½-inch (6-cm) Styrofoam ball

small round oatmeal box

two wiggle eyes

string or yarn

brown felt scraps

fiberfill

Here is what you do:

1 Cut the bottom out of the oatmeal box. Slide the sock over the box, so that the cuff opening of the sock just fits around the edge of the box. The box will be the groundhog's hole.

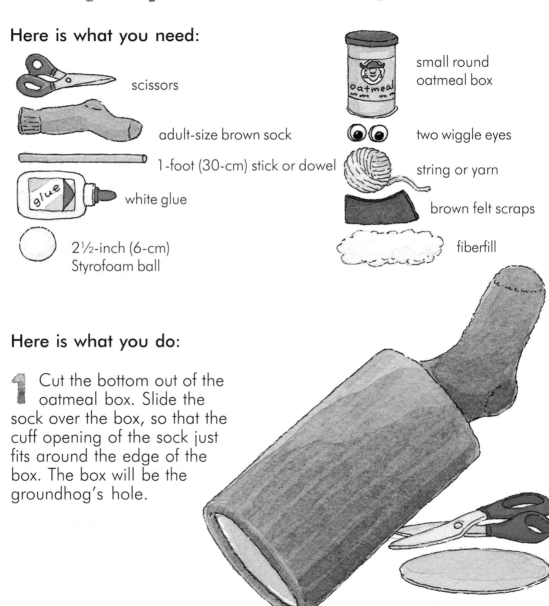

2 Dip one end of the stick in glue, then push it into the Styrofoam ball. Push the ball through the box and into the toe of the sock, with the stick coming out of the bottom of the box. The ball will be the head of the groundhog. Tie a piece of string around the stick at the base of the Styrofoam ball to make the groundhog's neck.

3 Glue the two wiggle eyes on one side of the head. Cut ears and a nose from the brown felt and glue them in place.

4 Glue fiberfill around the top rim of the box for snow.

Push on the stick to pop your groundhog up out of the hole to see if he sees his shadow. If he sees it, pull on the stick to put him back in his hole for six more weeks of winter. "Oh, no!"

43)

Surprise someone special on Valentine's Day with this sweet-smelling project.

Hanging Potpourri

Here is what you need:

metal lid from frozen juice container

ruler

scissors

thin ribbon

masking tape

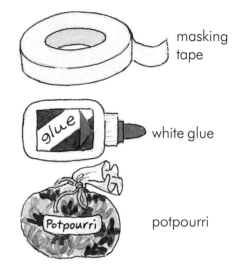

white glue

potpourri

Here is what you do:

1 Cover the indented side of the lid with masking tape to create a better gluing surface.

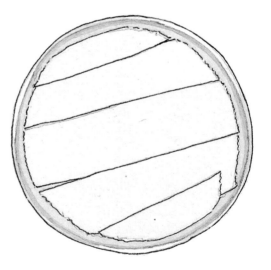

2 Cut a 10-inch (25-cm) length of ribbon to use for a hanger. Tape the two ends of the ribbon over the masking-taped side of the lid.

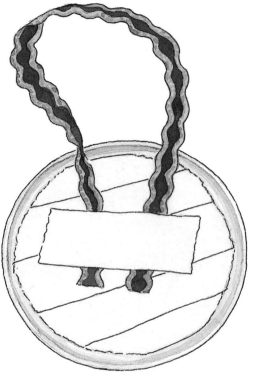

3 Cover the taped side of the lid with glue. Immediately press potpourri into the glue to completely cover the lid. Let the glue dry.

This little ornament will make any room smell sweeter.

45)

Make this heart carrier for all of your valentine mail.

Heart Mail Carrier

Here is what you need:

 scissors

red construction paper

 pencil

white glue

 large cereal box

red yarn

 ruler

pretty rickrack, lace, or other trims

Here is what you do:

1 Cut the corner from the bottom of the box so that the side of the box is the same length as the bottom of the box. The open side of the triangle will be the top of your heart carrier.

2 Use a pencil to trace around one edge of the box on the red paper. Cut around the tracing, leaving an extra inch of paper on each side. Cut a second piece of paper the same size to cover the other edge of the triangle.

46)

3 Trace around the two sides of the point of the box. Turn the drawing into a heart by drawing two bumps on the top. Cut out a heart shape for each side of the box.

4 Cover the entire outside of the box with glue. Glue the side papers on each edge of the box, folding the extra paper down over the sides of the box. Trim off any extra paper.

5 Glue a heart to the front and the back of the box.

6 Decorate the heart with pretty trims. Use the trims to make your initials in the center of the heart on one side of the carrier.

7 Punch a hole in the top edge of each side of the heart box. Cut two 18-inch (46-cm) pieces of yarn. String a piece through each hole, then bring all four ends of the yarn up to the center above the heart and tie them to make a handle for the carrier.

This heart carrier looks pretty hanging up when not in use.

47)

Bird Valentine

Here is what you need:

pencil

red, yellow, and pink construction paper

scissors

two wiggle eyes

white glue

black marker

Here is what you do:

1 Use the pencil to trace your two hands and one foot on the red paper. Trace your other foot on the yellow paper. Cut out the outlines of your hands and feet.

2 To make the beak for the bird, bend the yellow foot in half.

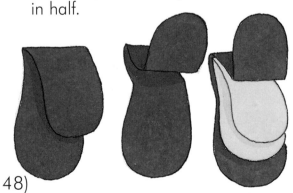

3 The body of the bird will be the red foot with the heel as the head. Bend the heel of the foot forward. Bend the heel up and the foot down to form a small slot to glue in the beak. Glue the beak in place.

48)

4 Glue a hand shape sticking out from each side of the body to make wings for the bird.

5 Cut two legs for the bird from the yellow paper. Glue the top of each leg to the bottom back side of the bird so that they hang down from the bottom of the bird.

6 Glue the two wiggle eyes to the head of the bird.

BACK

FRONT

7 Cut a heart from the pink paper small enough to fit inside the bird's mouth. Use the marker to write a valentine message on the heart. Glue the heart inside the bird's mouth.

Be Mine! Love Kathy

You might want to punch a hole in the top of your bird and tie on a piece of red yarn so that you can hang the bird up.

49)

Candy Magnet

Here is what you need:

 masking tape

 sticky-back magnet

 white glue

 1-inch (2½-cm) pom-pom in a yummy color

 colored glue

empty brown-pleated candy wrapper

Here is what you do:

1 Put a small piece of masking tape over the bottom inside of the candy wrapper to create a better gluing surface. Glue the pom-pom inside the wrapper to look like a piece of candy.

2 Decorate the top of the candy with dribbles of colored glue.

3 Put a piece of sticky-back magnet on the bottom of the candy wrapper.

Several of these candy magnets in a decorated box would make a very nice gift for Valentine's Day.

51)

Celebrate President's Day by making a hat like one that was worn by our first president . . .

George Washington Hat

Here is what you need:

 two pieces of 12- by 18-inch (30- by 46-cm) blue construction paper

 ruler

scissors

 masking tape

white glue

 plastic gallon milk jug for drying

 foil cupcake wrapper

 paintbrush

 pencil

 red ribbon

Here is what you do:

1 Stack the two sheets of blue paper together. Fold the sheets of paper in half to make four layers of paper 9 by 12 inches (23 by 30 cm). Cut the corner off each side, making a 10-inch (25-cm)-long cut from each corner of the folded side to the top center of the paper. Starting at the center of the folded side, cut a 6-inch (15-cm) slit up the triangle shape.

2 Open the two layers of folded paper to get a hat. The slit in the hat should fit over the top of your head.

52)

3 The two layers will need to be glued together. Put a small piece of masking tape at the end of each slit of each layer. Put the tape on the bottom side of the top layer and the top side of the bottom layer so that the tape will be in between the two layers and not show.

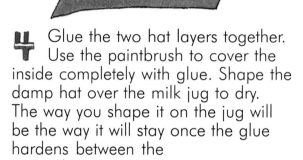

4 Glue the two hat layers together. Use the paintbrush to cover the inside completely with glue. Shape the damp hat over the milk jug to dry. The way you shape it on the jug will be the way it will stay once the glue hardens between the paper layers.

5 Flatten the foil cupcake wrapper to use for a medallion for the hat. Put a piece of masking tape on one side of the foil to create a better gluing surface. Cut a 12-inch (30-cm) piece of red ribbon. Fold the ribbon in half at an angle. Glue the folded end of the ribbon behind the foil so that the ends of the ribbon hang down. Put a piece of masking tape over the glued ribbon. Glue the medallion to one side of the hat.

Put on the hat and pretend you are sailing across the Delaware.

53)

Abraham Lincoln Mask

Here is what you need:

 9-inch (23-cm) paper plate

 scissors

newspaper to work on

 stapler

 black construction paper

 white glue

 black poster paint and a paintbrush

Here is what you do:

1 Cut the center out of the paper plate. Paint the entire back of the rim of the plate black for Abe's beard.

2 Cut a 7- by 8-inch (18- by 20-cm) piece of black paper for the hat. Glue a 7-inch (18-cm) side of the paper to the edge of the black rim beard.

3 Cut a 2- by 12-inch (5- by 30-cm) strip of black paper for the rim of the hat. Glue the strip across the bottom of the hat.

4 Cut a strip of black paper to make a band for the back of the mask to hold it in place. Staple one end of the strip to one side of the mask behind the base of the hat. Fit the strip to your head, then staple the other end in place.

Do you know why Mr. Lincoln was such an important president?

55)

Freezing temperatures are needed to make this beautiful outdoor decoration.

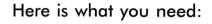
Icy Sun Catcher

Here is what you need:

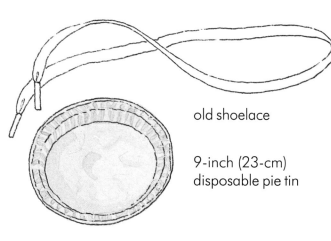

old shoelace

9-inch (23-cm) disposable pie tin

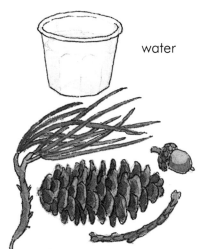

water

natural materials such as pinecones, pine needles, and twigs

Here is what you do:

1 Fold the shoelace in half and place the two ends across the center of the pie tin.

2 Make an arrangement of natural materials in the tin.

56)

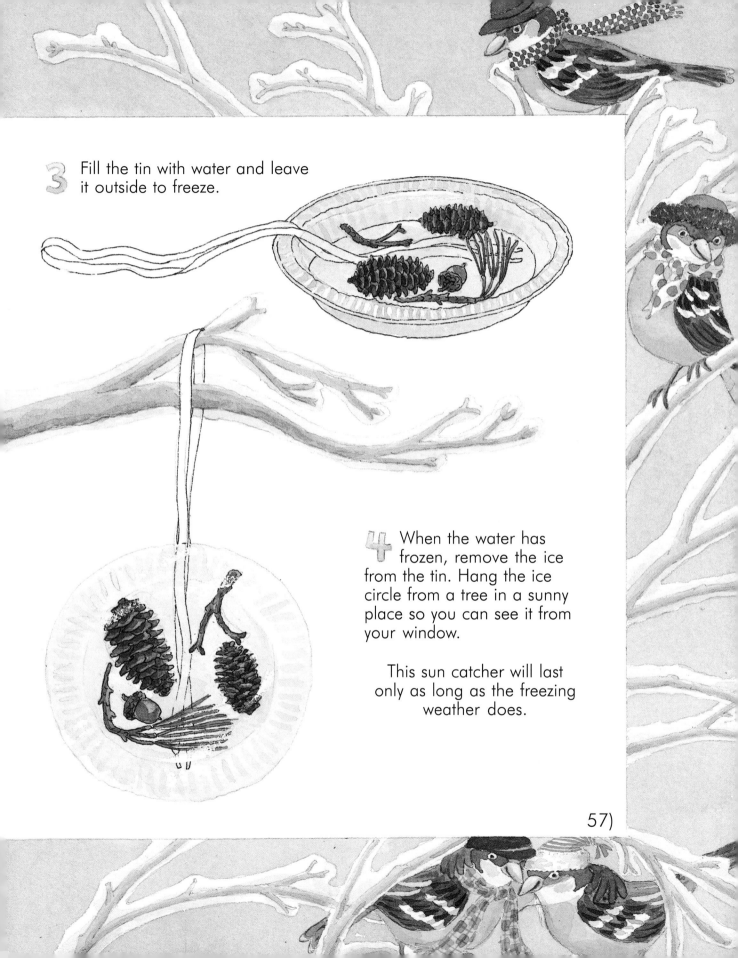

3 Fill the tin with water and leave it outside to freeze.

4 When the water has frozen, remove the ice from the tin. Hang the ice circle from a tree in a sunny place so you can see it from your window.

This sun catcher will last only as long as the freezing weather does.

57)

Celebrate Purim with a King Ahasuerus or Queen Esther treat holder.

Purim Treat Holder

Here is what you need:

white glue

scissors

masking tape

paper fastener

three 9-ounce plastic cups in two or three different colors

two wiggle eyes

black yarn

marker

metallic trim

Here is what you do:

1 Cut away about one third of the side of one cup. Turn it upside down and place it over a cup of a different color to look like a cape. This will be the body of the figure.

2 Cut the top two thirds of the last cup into points to look like a crown.

3 Wrap the remaining base of the cup with masking tape to make a head beneath the crown.

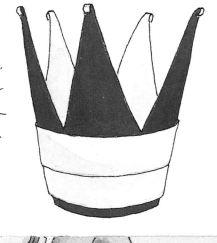

58)

4 Poke a hole through the center of the bottom of the head cup. Poke a hole through the bottom of the two cups that form the body. Attach the head to the body using a paper fastener placed through the holes in the cups.

5 Glue black yarn hair on the head. If you are making the king cup, glue on a beard also. Glue on two wiggle eyes. Use the markers to add any other facial features you wish.

6 Glue metallic trim around the base of the crown above the hair.

Fill the crown with candy treats and give it to someone special for Purim.

59)

February is National Dental Health month.

Happy Teeth Finger Puppets

Here is what you need:

 markers

 scissors

 white glue

red construction paper

 three 9-inch (23-cm) paper plates in skin color of choice

 stapler

 old white glove

 yarn for hair

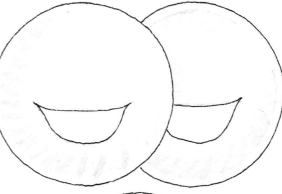

Here is what you do:

1 Draw an open mouth about 4 inches (10 cm) long and 2½ inches (6 cm) wide on the back of one paper plate. Cut the mouth area out.

2 Trace the open mouth on the back of a second paper plate and cut that mouth out too. The second plate will go under the first plate.

3 Use the markers to draw lips around the open mouth on the first plate. Also, draw eyes and a nose.

60)

4 Cut the thumb and the pinkie finger from the glove. Staple the two pieces hanging down from the top of the open mouth of the second plate so that they look like teeth.

5 Cut the remaining three fingers from the glove, leaving them attached at the base of the fingers. Staple the fingers sticking up like bottom teeth from the open mouth of the uncolored plate. Staple only one side of the base of the glove so that you can slip your fingers into the teeth to wiggle them.

6 Use the markers to draw a happy face on each tooth.

7 Staple the face plate to the plate with the teeth on the top and each side of the face.

8 Glue red paper over the top (eating side) of the third paper plate. Put the face plate over the paper-covered plate so that the red paper shows behind the mouth. Staple the plates together on the sides and the top.

9 Cut yarn bits for hair. Glue the yarn hair around the face.

Slip your fingers into the bottom teeth and have them remind everyone to brush their teeth so they will have happy teeth too.

Sprout a Pet

Here is what you need:

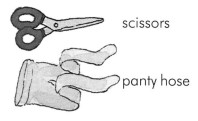 scissors

panty hose

 hairpin

plastic food storage bag

 birdseed

 potting soil

 two thumbtacks

 water

Here is what you do:

1 Cut one leg off the panty hose. Fill the foot of the stocking leg with potting soil. Shake the soil-filled stocking gently to help the dirt settle, then add a little more to fill in the foot area.

2 Slide birdseed into the foot between the stocking and the dirt. Try to cover as much of the dirt with seed as you can.

3 Knot the stocking just above the foot to hold the dirt in place. Loop the excess stocking over and knot it to make a hanger for the dirt-filled foot.

4 Put the two thumbtacks in the toe end of the foot for eyes. Slide one end of the hairpin through the top of the head and spread the two ends to look like antennae.

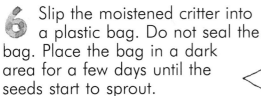

5 Moisten the seeds with water. A plant mister or spray bottle would be perfect for this job.

6 Slip the moistened critter into a plastic bag. Do not seal the bag. Place the bag in a dark area for a few days until the seeds start to sprout.

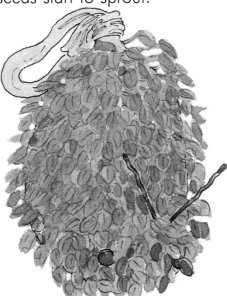

7 When the seeds have sprouted, hang your critter in a window and keep it moist.

You might want to design your own creature. You can use anything for details that will slip through the stocking material. Try using pipe cleaners or map pins to add details.

63)

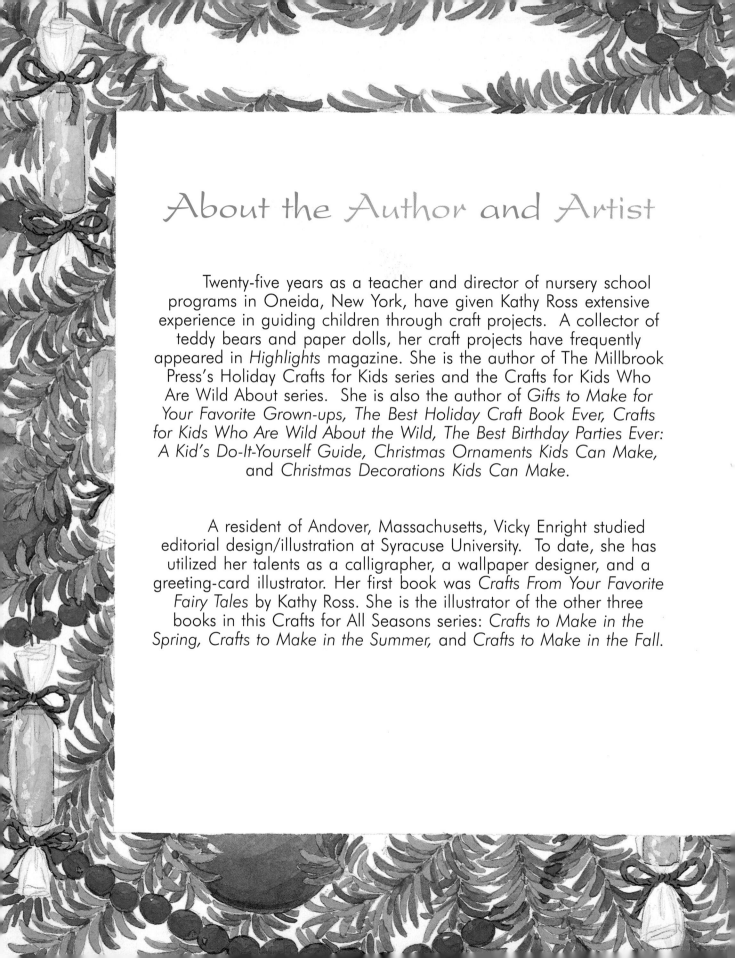

About the Author and Artist

Twenty-five years as a teacher and director of nursery school programs in Oneida, New York, have given Kathy Ross extensive experience in guiding children through craft projects. A collector of teddy bears and paper dolls, her craft projects have frequently appeared in *Highlights* magazine. She is the author of The Millbrook Press's Holiday Crafts for Kids series and the Crafts for Kids Who Are Wild About series. She is also the author of *Gifts to Make for Your Favorite Grown-ups, The Best Holiday Craft Book Ever, Crafts for Kids Who Are Wild About the Wild, The Best Birthday Parties Ever: A Kid's Do-It-Yourself Guide, Christmas Ornaments Kids Can Make,* and *Christmas Decorations Kids Can Make.*

A resident of Andover, Massachusetts, Vicky Enright studied editorial design/illustration at Syracuse University. To date, she has utilized her talents as a calligrapher, a wallpaper designer, and a greeting-card illustrator. Her first book was *Crafts From Your Favorite Fairy Tales* by Kathy Ross. She is the illustrator of the other three books in this Crafts for All Seasons series: *Crafts to Make in the Spring, Crafts to Make in the Summer,* and *Crafts to Make in the Fall.*